To Kathleen

2.99

Red Landscapes

Keep on writing!

Mike Jenks
?

To Marie, Bethan and Ciaran, with love.

Mike Jenkins
Red Landscapes
new and selected poems

seren

seren
is the book imprint of
Poetry Wales Press Ltd
Wyndham Street, Bridgend, Wales

ISBN 1-85411-244-9

A CIP record for this title is available from
the British Library

*The publisher works with the financial assistance of the
Arts Council of Wales*

Cover : 'Red Landscape' by Geoffrey Olsen

Printed in Palatino by WBC Book Manufacturers, Bridgend

Contents

from
The Common Land

Chartist Meeting

Heolgerrig, 1842

The people came to listen
looking down valley as they tramped;
the iron track was a ladder
from a loft to the open sea —
salt filling the air like pollen.

Each wheel was held fast
as you would grip a coin;
yet everything went away from them.
The black kernel of the mountains
seemed endless, but still in their stomachs
a furnace-fire roared,
and their children's eyes hammered
and turned and hollowed out a cannon.

Steam was like a spiral of wool
threaded straight down the valley,
lost past a colliery.
The tramways held the slope
as though they were wood of a pen.
Wives and children were miniatures
of the hill, the coal ingrained
in enclosures on their skin.

They shook hands with the sky,
an old friend; there, at the field,
oak trees turned to crosses
their trunks bent with the weight
of cloud and wind, and harsh grass
from marshes that Morgan Williams,
the weaver, could raise into a pulpit.

A thousand listened, as way below them
Cyfarthfa Castle was set like a diamond
in a ring of green,
and the stalks of chimneys
bloomed continuous smoke and flame.

The Welsh that was spoken
chuckled with streams, plucked bare rock,
and men like Morgan Williams
saw in the burnt hands a harvest of votes.

A Truant

Looking down on the open-cast pit,
a black crater, with tracks coiled
like an electrical circuit,
and yellow trucks like remote-controlled toys.
Sheer cliff blasted out has given
the mountain many spasms of shock.

With biscuit tin for his companion, we meet him,
the nightwatchman. Where he lived the nettles
and bracken root out the foundation.
His words lay bare the seam below our feet,
obstinate coal which can touch men like a plague—
the moonscape recedes beneath his peaked cap.

As if there were no fences or danger signs
he invites us to enter, as if the whole mountainside
were his parlour. He tells of pensioners
trying to hide behind the winter dark
as they snuffled out lumps of coal —
led them home along the path in his own boot-prints.

"Welsh lagoons there!" he says, "even the weeping
of the dead miners is black". I look again
at the bush-browed ponds of pumped water,
to Aberdare in the pocket of the hills
and then at the man, out whinberry-picking,
a truant from the narrow streets of the town.

My Gran

My Gran feeds the cat
on bits of cheese,
on bits of chocolate biscuit
crumbled up;
the cat isn't very pleased.
She calls her "Pussy Puss" —
sometimes she calls the cushion
by the same name.

My Gran burns kettles,
burns meals-on-wheels,
has been known to burn
a hole in her dress;
accuses the Home Help
of stealing her handkerchiefs.
Finds hankies, and washes them
dirtier than they were before.

My Gran falls through the floor
every morning, needs cups of tea
to bring her round to insanity,
needs glasses of sherry
to help her forget
that she can't remember.
Phones the butcher
to phone the doctor.

Lays tea at five
and supper at nine,
asks her dead husband
the time of year,
the day of time.
Blocks her bedroom door
with a bulky bureau
which screams every night
like a ghost.

My Gran likes only one
piece of toast
for tea and breakfast.

My Gran plays patience
and cheats,
drinks only one glass
of sherry a day,
and two bottles in half a week.
Threatens to have me turned out,
to call the police.

She's mad, I think,
or the clocks have stopped.

from
Empire of Smoke

Memorials

There are men with rising-damp in their bones,
men with germs working double-shifts and overtime
in their veins, men whose mouths
could outdrink their brains,
whose hearts sack the rest of their bodies.

There are women about to give birth
to washing-machines, women whose blue-mould
bruises are painted over with make-up,
who take pills because of chronic discrimination,
who catch cancer from watching too much television.

I came here looking for an answer to sleep —
my mind at nights travelling into exile.
Will they sever the trail
from the stomach of the Depression?
Will they stitch up the deep cuts
left when thousands had to leave this town?

They built a warehouse of graves
in Pant, to store the bodies which had been
dipped into the stench-filled crucible
of Lord Cholera's finest possession.

What memorial will we have?
Streets named after Dic Penderyn and Wellington
squaring up both sides of the valley
alive only with wandering dogs?

I

I is the biggest word
in the English language —
some people yawn bored
as soon as you mention it.

I know people who erect crosses
made from it
and then refuse to carry them.

I know people who build extensions
onto it and call
those extensions their children.

I know people who would
like to keep changing it
every week like fashionable clothing.

I know people who hate it so much
it's become an obsession,
like a priest always ranting against sin.

In English, "I" begins the sentence:
the other words queue up behind it
waiting for their instructions.

You must write "I" with a capital letter
but "we" with a small one.
Why?... well... as in God and Great Britain.

i know a person who tries to make it
mock itself, to disguise an ambition.
i know a person who thinks it will outlive
the exploring body, the inflated mind.

"He Loved Light, Freedom and Animals"

*An inscription on the grave of one of the children who
died in the Aberfan disaster of October 21st, 1966.*

No grave could contain him.
He will always be young
in the classroom
waving an answer
like a greeting.

Buried alive —
alive he is
by the river
skimming stones down
the path of the sun.

When the tumour on the hillside
burst and the black blood
of coal drowned him,
he ran forever
with his sheepdog leaping
for sticks, tumbling together
in windblown abandon.

I gulp back tears
because of a notion of manliness.
After the October rain
the slag-heap sagged
its greedy coalowner's belly.
He drew a picture of a wren,
his favourite bird for frailty
and determination. His eyes gleamed
as gorse-flowers do now
above the village.

His scream was stopped mid-flight.
Black and blemished
with the hill's sickness
he must have been,
like a child collier
dragged out of one of Bute's mines —
a limp statistic.

There he is, climbing a tree,
mimicking an ape, calling out names
at classmates. Laughs springing
down the slope. My wife hears them
her ears attuned as a ewe's in lambing.
and I try to foster the inscription,
away from its stubborn stone.

Laughter Tangled in Thorn

Dressed like a child
for our ritual Sunday afternoon
pilgrimage to the hillside:
your pear-shaped hood,
scarf wound like a snake
and red ski-boots dragged along
like grown-up things worn for a dare.

When I laugh, I don't mean it to hurt.
It is the brother of the laugh
at the end of our love-making —
rigid bones melting into blood.

The moor grass has turned
into a frosty yellow, its green
gone deep into hibernation.
We crunch mud, step streams,
in games which strip us of years
like the trees have been
of their leaves. The water
and your green eyes
share the only motion.

You see a red berry
and call it a ladybird.
I think of your city upbringing;
the seasons being passing strangers
through Belfast streets
where you cadged rides from the ice.

When the brook's chatter is snow-fed,
your laughter is tangled in thorn.
You discover an ice sculpture
mounted on a spine of reed,
and call it "Teeth and Jaws".
The light of your words
travels through it.

High above Merthyr, mountain lapping mountain.
You are amazed at the rarefied sunlight!
When you speak, the numb streets
are startled. We leave the childhood
of the moorland, to grow taller
with a tiredness which is the sister
of when we lie, translucent and still,
on the single spine of our bed.

Discovering

Horizontal dancing
to the sound
of the spinning earth —
vulnerable as
a frantic fly
yet ready to burst
from the house's pod.

With you, we discover
senses
that logic's
data banks
had tried to process
into the pure expression.

Paper flaps like giant ferns
and there is a cave
in the corner of the room.
It is possible
to pick up
shards of shadows
to make into tools.

And when your hunger-screams
fly in the primeval forest
they are
half-lizard, half-bird.

Neighbours

Yesterday, the children made the street
into a stadium; their cat
a docile audience. As they cheered
a score, it seemed there was a camera
in the sky to record their elation.

Men polished cars, like soldiers
getting ready for an inspection.
Women, of course, were banished
from daylight: the smells of roasts merging
like the car-wash channels joining.

Today, two horses trespass over boundaries
of content; barebacked, as if they'd just
thrown off the saddle of some film.
They hoof up lawns — brown patches like tea-stains.
They nudge open gates with a tutored nose.

A woman in an apron tries to sweep away
the stallion, his penis wagging back at her broom.
I swop smiles with an Indian woman, door to door.
These neighbours bring us out from our burrows —
the stampede of light watering our eyes.

from
Invisible Times

Canine Graffiti

Some loopy boy wrote "FUCK OFF"
in firm felt-tip on the white back
of a nippy-as-a-ferret Jack Russell.

Senior Staff spotted it while it shat
in the midst of a modern dance
formation — leotards snapped!

(When they weren't busy piercing ears
with sharp instructions, or spiking hair
with swift backhand cuffs,

they did have time to snoop on lessons
which exceeded the statutory decibel rate.)
They set off in pursuit of the errant dog,

skilfully hurdling its poop in the process.
They chased it into Mathematics
where it caused havoc by lifting a leg

45° towards the blackboard's right-angle.
Then through the Audio-Visual concepts room,
across a film of *Henry V*, making Olivier's horse

rear and throw the bewildered actor.
It hid behind a smoke-screen in the bogs,
sniffed out bunkers in the coal-bunker.

For hours it disappeared and Senior Staff
suspected a trendy English teacher
of using it as an aid to creative writing.

Finally it was duly discovered
by Lizzie Locust (Biology), necking
with a stuffed stoat in the store-cupboard.

Now you can see the distraught Headmistress
scrubbing from bell to bell in her office,
a small dog held down by burly, sweating prefects.

Orange-Peel Man

Small man from up the Rhymni Valley
stunted to the size
of a mining-gallery.
Silver hair the shine
of a butty-can.
Walks with a limp:
no compensation.

Every other Saturday's
relegation struggle, among
moaners and masochists,
behind the tallest pine-tree fans
he stands. Shouts
at the players like a trainer.

Might as well be in blind-black
at the seam, for all he can see:
yet he knows who has the ball
(invariably the opposition!)
and flings, disgusted, orange-peel
at players who ignore his tactics,
whose wages weigh the same as him.

Industrial Museum

for Adrian Mitchell

Hello and welcome to our industrial museum.

On your right there's a slag-heap reclaimed...
a hill... another slag-heap...
that one shaped as a landing-pad
for bird-like hang-gliders.

Notice the pit-wheels perfectly preserved
where you can buy mementoes
of the big Strike and eat authentic cawl
at an austere soup-kitchen.

There mummified miners cough and spit
at the press of a button
and you can try their lungs on
to a tape-recording of Idris Davies' poems.

That rubble was a 19th century chapel,
that pile of bricks an industrial estate.
The terraced houses are all adorned
in red, white and blue as if royalty were visiting.

See how quaint the wax models
of women are, as they bow in homage
to polished doorsteps, the stuffed sheep
at the roadside give off a genuine odour.

The graveyards have been covered over
and lounge-chairs provided for viewing
gravestones which tell of deaths from cholera
or pit explosions. I recommend their cafeterias.

In the ruins of the Town Hall the council
give public performances, meeting
to discuss the valley's future:
their *hwyl* is high and *hiraeth* higher.

Finally, let's visit the Foot Arms
(in memory of a long-gone leader)
and listen to the last Valley's character
who lives here, courtesy of the Welsh Office, in a tin bath.

Nant Gwrtheyrn

Perched on a grassy ledge,
like some rare sea-birds we feel;
learning the language of an endangered species.

And whatever the reasons that brought us,
the sea shelves at the edge
of our thoughts and the mountains
mouse our trivialities. Shaggy, purple head
of the lying yet waiting peninsula.

The wind's descant and harp-curves
of branches, together in penillion.
Candles are toadstools turned into a rage
of horses by Gwydion's flames.
I am dumb: my mind full of knelling
calls of quarrymen, pulled by the waves' ropes.

Wild goats tread the cliff-path
between reality and myth.
Shy and wary behind a twmp:
hear their night-time rock-fall
as they move in to graze
on pastures which pit beyond our step.

I watch the gradual renovation:
my learning tractored across rough ground
and voice beginning to fit the rhythm
of the carpenter as I feel
around and around, the eddying of Yr Iaith.

See, the granite lies in piles of nuggets
where no boat will beach.
High up to the mountain-top
the stone-supports hoist only cloud.

Listen how we talk and how the sea
rolls boulders from its tongue.

John

The sting of the fumes
and petrol had bloodshot his eyes
so they looked like an alcoholic's.
"Sir" was a word he'd abolished.
He only stooped to tend a car.
He saw bosses come and go
with fashions. In all weathers
he took his time.

His cap at a witty angle,
breaktimes we'd crouch together
secret sharers of the showroom.
Our ideas travelled further
than any of those pampered
cars could ever go.

His Valley's voice rising
to mountain-air elation —
falling to chatty river-flow.
He spoke of the Depression:
how he'd trudged on blistering feet
grey miles, a mirage of bread
becoming real ahead of him.

Some months after I'd left,
an old workmate, cool as coins,
told me of his fatal heart-attack.
A chosen son, I walked
at his own funeral pace
from the garage towards
a rusting distance I'd never attain.

Meeting Mrs Bernstein

Mrs Bernstein, the dogs sniff suspiciously
in your plotted neighbourhood,
while you open your door and your life
to strangers: trying to sell us your house
when we came for a piano;
sprightly body nudging a doddering mind.

You introduce us to your husband
who, impassively from the sideboard,
remains your dear boy.
With your father, the town's last rabbi,
your pride is framed.
In a small drawer
is tucked away your profession.

"Here they all are!" you say.
On a table's planet
the seas and cities defined
in pictures of your family.
Confident fathers and dark-skinned
daughters explained by qualifications.

Incongruous amongst a trilled dresser
and desk where you drum out the past
are Harvard and Yale pennants:
two sails beckoning your sight
beyond the whispering walls.

Mrs Bernstein, we listen to your playing:
Rachmaninov's chords bluster to America
where your anger declares itself;
during Chopin's night you commune
with your restless dead.

Down the garden steps you grip my hand
with a ring of bone. We cannot buy
this instrument of emotions
only your fingers know.

Fool of the Fields

Hair as wild as his arms,
growing in all directions
at once, like ubiquitous weeds
over acres of wasteland.

Expert at impersonations
he sent a dreary lesson
flying with his imitation
of a mother giving birth.

He went to school
just to bunk lessons;
teachers tried to break him in
but he broke their voices.

He scratched himself at the wrong times
in all the wrong places
and though girls said he was honking
they laughed tears at his jokes.

Even the really rock boys
were wary of his tinder-eyes
and with the Magic Mushroom crop
he was dubbed "Fool of the Fields".

Who could tell that behind
those pecking hands, that half-moon smile
was his mother, visited by endless nightmares
under the numbing lights of an asylum?

Survivor

They came from the arterial streets
of Dowlais, to the pill-box estate
wired to the hillside. Married
too young, for their bodies' sake.

You were, at first, a novelty
won at a fair. Then you cried
every night, dragging them from calm
of a deep sleep like a premature
birth again and again...
until he learnt to slumber and snore
nailed by bottles to his marriage-bed.
You grew up doing the opposite
of all the examples they set.

Now you smile survival at me,
like one of those old Dowlais buildings:
the Library propped by scaffolding
(friends hold you steady).
If I looked long enough
into the archives of your mind
perhaps I'd find the reason.

The time your father's bayonet-case
came down like a truncheon
onto your mother, you couldn't hide
behind their smoke or fan the fire
any longer. You hit his helmet-head,
so he struck out and you lay
like an imitation of the dead.

Tracey — the common name belies you.
You have reclaimed the black hills
of night with your boys on stolen bikes.
The sound of their engines
worries round and round your mother
as she sits and knits alone.
Your father's in a cot
crazily shaking its bars.

Dic Dywyll

I have banished God
further than the Antipodes
since my so-called accident.
He was the owner
of those mills of death,
his manager the old Cholera.
The preaching of Cheapjack remedies:
holding up heaven as a cure.

They took my eyes
and struck them
into cannon-balls.
My mask and its perpetual night
is known to the pit-ponies.

Crossing the Iron Bridge
I hear the river's voice
bring tune to my ballads,
the hooves of canal-horses
count beats and pauses come
as I breathe the welcome wind
from the west and eventual sea.

Night arrives and they all
share my mask: punchy drunkards,
rousing rebels and laughing ones
who sup to conquer daytime.

My daughter is the blackbird
giving flames to the begging hearth
of our basement with her song;

and I am the owl, I turn
to face their sufferings,
call them out to chase away
the chimneys' shadows. Masters
I magic to mice
under the death's-head moon.

Note: Dic Dywyll was a renowned balladeer in nineteenth-century
Merthyr, who was blinded working at the Crawshay ironworks.
His daughter, Myfanwy, was immortalised in Joseph Parry's song.

Among Shoals of Stars

Each night the sea
tires of its slopping and slapping
and ascends the limestone staircase
of cactus-sharp stone.

It lies down
where sky has been,
waving away the blue
and only hooded clouds
show its occasional restlessness.

Bright fish with mouths
that globe look down on me
and the breezy wish-wish
of sea-weed is the needled
branches of every pine.

I see the lights
of planes as they are out
trawling for dreams.
The moon spills milk
which I drink in,
before I too lie down
to sleep among shoals of stars.

Stallion

When the night's stallion
approaches us over the yellowing fields,
we see shafts of loneliness
in his eyes. The last wild flowers
have gone with the mares
he whinnied to, over the high-barred gate.

A barbed mockery of thorn-trees
and the two of us — jesting to catch
leaves feathering down — share
the hillside with the coal-hewn stallion.

Once, he had broken free, his spine
bridging the moor and the village,
hooves clicking the tongues of sleep.
Now, pushing flanks against staked branches,
he mules his raked flesh.

Invisible Times

Living in invisible times:
loneliness an economist's art.

Into the phone I take care:
testing the colour of each word
because of the spy whose wire
antennas twitch, whose mouth
is a metal tube my voice falls down
to be shred like paper.

Outside, I wear a crustaceous coat,
knowing that the rain avenges
those gun-barrel chimneys
who wage war on the sky.
One day my scales will be eaten away
and flesh frazzled to cinders.

All around are the sick people
who cannot find the germs.
I tell them where to look:
under switches which grow on fingertips,
in clocks whose hands are trees
and pylons and flags.

Every day I'm on this journey:
looking for the computer who told
those lies, who caused my rejection.
"Facts are seeds grown hard
as bullets," I would inform it.
But my search is aimless,
because the computer whirrs
in too many skulls to crack open.

The expert tells me I'm mad.
I see the motorway that workmen
are laying behind his grin:
it runs from the city of emotion
to the city of reason
and all purpose is within its rims.

from
A Dissident Voice

Creature

Last night the sea heaved up a creature,
one I could not explain.

Half-boat, half-animal it seemed:
ribs of rusted tin, skull smooth as plastic.

My daughter played in its house of bones,
bouncing pebbles like syllables ringing.

She kept asking its name, how old was it?
Was it a dragon? Oil like blood dripped.

"I don't know!" I said (sounding unscientific):
she pulled out bolts of its neck to sit on.

I pursued it in books: the Bible dumb.
She ran in and out of its tunnel of questions.

Woman on Wheels

Don't look down on me!
I'm a remarkable invention:
half-vehicle and half-human!

Don't joke about such things?
Well, what is there left?
God's deserted me,
or I've ignored him....
whatever, it's neither blame nor salvation.

Don't look away or speak slowly,
I only grin stupidly
when I've taken too much gin.

Later, in the morning,
messages from my brain
jam in my throat.
My spine's a street
I can only walk in sleep
or in those photos once placed
in a case too high to reach.

Running on smoke not steam,
I become the mechanic
as I take my leg from the cupboard
to put on as you would make-up.
I prefer to numb myself
in poison-clouds of my making,
rather than face a sun
shining like instruments of operation.

You think I'm not like you?
It's true the world is full
of stairs and people climbing,

while I remain below
locked into pavement, gazing
as the building saunters away.

Yet I know some who are paralysed within,
so all they've achieved
becomes a throbbing, an ache
from a lost limb.

Our Living-Room Parliament

Sitting in that cube of smoke:
your friend on a cushion of papers,
the women puffing in unison.
The fire spat out sparks,
while TV sportsmen
mimed to no ovations.

You and I on the edge of hard chairs,
balancing debate: our living-room
parliament. To finish a sentence
you'd slice atmosphere with remarks.

Cream-cakes and tea, reminiscences and jokes;
but always the wrangles we relished.
I disagreed... I learnt from you:
nothing Headmasterly-wrought
about the way you listened
as I decreed worker and worker
outside traditions of culture and creed.

As the pills are no longer numbing,
I see how you were right.
As you're being eaten away
with the paltry food you can take,
I taste those Saturdays
brought back by wheaten bread.

One afternoon, all our talking stopped.
The house shook as though trying
to rid itself of troubles.
Miles across a city a warehouse of evidence
rose into the sky and was lost.
You'd seen the batons come down
on heads which favoured thought.
You'd seen the gas put masks
on eyes which would take borders
seaward from the common source.

At a road-block once, faced by police
with machine-guns to shrivel pride,
you replied in Gaelic. They glared
and muttered, thinking you a lunatic.

I cannot describe your illness
as *pain*: that would be as simple
as the formula I had applied
to your nation's present and past.

You stand. You'll stand as long as you can.
I'll finish my sentence for you to retort.

An Escape

On the mantelpiece, my mother's trophies
stand in line and wink at me.
They collect any sunlight
in our shabby room, where carpet stains
are bruises... his jealousy
those dents she couldn't dust away.

My Mam's at work again, on the tills
handling all that money which flows
through her like the facts
they funnel into me at school.
Keeping the bailiffs from biting
harder than any Big Freeze.

I wipe the condensation with my sleeve:
its smear like snot. I peer
through a film of dirt and damp
at dog-packs worrying the bins.
They search and tear for scraps,
their hunger sharpening canines.
Find more than in our kitchen!

It's the rain I despise... nagging me inside
with memories of screaming, fighting:
"Oh no! Dad!"... "Get away you bastard son!"

But here comes Lisa with our dog
and her friends all wild in the wind;
and we're off to the little river,
to the tree-trunk bridge where our heads
will be leaf-light and reeling.

The Skin I Want

No more names:
no more "Rem! Rem!"
"His dad's a wog!"
"His dad fucks little girls!"

          I will rise myself up.
          I'll dive into a sea-dream
          where I'll breathe like a fish.

No more poke and taunt,
point, cackle, croak:
ganging around me, with
"Sly... sly... look at his curly black..."

          I will feel the rope
          a forgotten cord, meet
          the one guardian I can trust.

No more crying, no more fists
knotted in my throat and sweat
burning like ink when I work.
No more... "Why can't you be like...?"

          I will become someone else:
          make my branch of wire
          and my hill from a chair.

No more bulb bursting in my head,
glass piercing, painting the walls
with spatters of blood.

          I will turn out the light
          with a jerk of my neck.
          Make the darkness be
          the skin that I want.

A Newt in the Classroom

At first, I took it
for a plastic practical joke.

But she picked him up
and he walked, out of his aqua-sphere,
like a man on the moon.

I grasped the moment, as she had
the lizard: holding the idea by its tail.
We dissected him with words.
We passed him along rows
like a thought too icy to hold.

He was a clay god
each made in their image.
The sensitive Australian girl
railing against his imprisonment
in the grey box of her classroom.
The boy who tried to get inside
the skin so much he shrank
into a different dimension.
Too many calling him "cute";
mistrusting their senses, even
their over-exhausted sight.

Under the sun of our attention
he was rapidly drying up:
"Get water from the Lab!"
"No, she'll cut him up!"

By Friday, he had died.
Turned white as blank paper,
while our walls were covered
with creations glued on
like his tail sticking to your palm.

Cwmaman

i.m. Alun Lewis

It is his funeral we attend:
finally fixing him on a plaque.
The tent of the sky rends
and the pages of the hillside
turn as the light comes back.

Some know better: anticipate
the resurrection of the words.
Others hide beneath umbrellas:
the rain subduing a need
for scandal, a rummaging
in the pockets of the dead.

The shops are blacked out
by another war, a slow venom
seeping in like acid rain.
The trains of terraces
permanently forgotten in the sidings.

The people of his town
face a famine of the mind,
fighting an invasion of damp and dark,
huddled round the fire of their talk.

The dole is their jungle of trackless time.
Still, they climb above the mirror
which is polished, loaded and primed,
to the mountain... lover and lover
aware of the river inside.

From
This House, My Ghetto

Always the Ocean

For those of us born by the ocean
there will always be a listening,
an ear close to the ground
like an animal trailing.

I remember one night
I couldn't see anything of water
and I was sober as the stars,
yet below the traced paving-stones
and gushing up through cracks...
benches tilted, clouds rocked.
I was a vessel, filled full of it.

This town at the valley's head
I've adopted or it's adopted me:
wakes fan from the simple phrases
and often laughter can erode
the most resistant expressions.
Despite this, I'm following the river
along our mutual courses:

to the boy on a storm-beach
hopping from boulder to boulder
trying to mimic a mountain-goat;
to the young man sitting in a ring
of perfumed smoke by the castle,
gazing at strings of dolphins
plucked by the sleight-fingered sea.

A Strange Recognition

Aberystwyth

A coincidence of eyes,
a lightning vision
across tables. Our notes
plodded, the out-of-date
statistics fixing us to seats.

Your long brown hair
I'd drawn in imagination
before we ever met.
My hungover head
too heavy to prop
juddered with the shock
of a strange recognition.

***

Outside the edge of the dance
I watched you ceilidh, swing
wildly with waves beneath your feet.

When we met I wanted to hide
in your accent, yet you mimicked me
as if learning a different language.

In the library, your metal-rimmed glasses
framed your eyes downward, concentrated.
Away from shelved knowledge
we barely touched, I noticed
their green of sea in a certain light.

***

Huddled and holding against the night-tide,
along the winding promenade,
stepping gradually into each other's histories.

The spurt and spume of breakers
hitting the sea-walls,
heat from our words making faces glow.

I rode the wind as I'd done
when a boy on the mountain:
then you caught me stumbling.

I lifted you up into air
which rolled and rounded our years
as beach-pebbles are eroded.

***

The day after, I talked
of someone else the next summer,
teasing you with her name
and letters exhibited:
cruel reminders of impermanence.

You didn't tear with spite,
but clung on so tightly
I wanted to throw your hand
out across the bay,
knowing it would come back eventually.

***

In your flat exchanging tales
of relatives, like well-worn books:
you took me across the water
before I'd boarded a boat.

I collected your sayings
pressed by our lips:
making the bulbs shake,
floorboards creaking fears.

Our minds were ceiling-cameras:
a film director we both imagined
yelling "Cut... cut... cut!"
just at the crucial instant.

***

It was a long way down
from the grassy hollow
above the cliff, a fit for our bodies,
to a station platform
and chat about domesticities.

From the seagulls' calls sharp
as rock pinnacles, to a park duck
alighting on a fence so near
I faced it lens to beak!

There was no ring of stalks
to be knotted round your finger,
only a timetable to make,
shunting our agreement into place.

But wherever we clutched
we'd glimpse the edge
and a rough path ahead,
always wary of falling.

Belfast

All around us the city was turning
into dust with dark approaching:
white dust from fires,
black dust flaking from buildings,
churned into the air
by a worry of helicopters.

Nothing else seemed substantial there:
I snuggled close to your softness
and the sheets whispered.

I shrank in your shoulder's cusp,
drinking your milky tones,
parched with oppressive dryness.

All you'd taught me couldn't explain
the guns' long hollows
and the one deadly mistake.

***

You spoke for me in daylight.
I blocked off my throat
like the streets we encountered.
Though firesides flared banter, argument.

I searched for the right expressions
but you kept the map
inside your head,
aware of the worst threats.

Time I thought you'd hidden
the voice I needed
and I'd act the interrogator
to make you confess.

Before sleep, it knocked at my heart
to be let in and I knew then
why you leapt at an everyday explosion
of noise from door or pan.

***

A mat of cheques
on the Presbytery floor.

If only your tears
had made the ink run
and blur, become a fog
of figures for a puzzled bishop.

They sentenced us there,
gave us "Twelve months! No more!"
They tore up our documents
as if that's all we were.

Your family owned one brick
of the parish church.
In a place where names and colours
could be a crime, we decided to make
our own banners and search
for a renegade who'd accept
the heresy of a love condemned.

***

I believe it was that first
union of looks, or further back
to that part of our selves
where opposites had been built:
good and evil, right and wrong,
brick above true contact's soil.

Not a vow or signature
nor legal paper with single name,
not a ring of precious metal
nor a hired suit for the occasion,
not a black limousine one citizen
rightly met with a two-finger salute.

Careless of your earnest whiteness
I wanted to strip the veil.
I was actor and commentator
at the stage of the altar.
Priests and congregation embraced
at the renegade's bidding.

What I want to remember is speeding
towards the border, joke-sprung,
lost in Free Derry in our rickety car;
towards a wilderness of coast and bogland,
heading for horizons as they surely darkened.

The Memory Dance

i.m. Philip Greagsby

"Anything strange or startling?"
your catchphrase over the phone:
with few of the heavy steps
of your adopted home.

In an armchair, made higher by papers,
you sat under a blanket of print
snoozing with the radio on in case
something happened round the corner.

Your best friend, the ace reporter,
used to take you with him as scribe,
yet you never wrote us letters.
Now you're the only news that matters.

Leaving food to rot, the car's haphazard,
we drive off into the night
and encounter a frightened fox, dazzled:
his nocturnal sight we borrowed.

I cry as we descend the mountain,
the city so much less for your leaving.
I must meet you for the last time:
lying, not an ink-bruise to be seen.

Against tradition, we carry you, men and women
away from the path and over weedspread stones,
away from communal plots whose names
you'd have tallied with a clerk's precision.

Ringing's no longer an ambulance siren.
Your elegant long-hand is waltzing
in your diary, to a gentler tone:
the memory dance has its own time.

The Lodger

The three children swooped on the letters:
dark-haired boy, eldest one, the dealer
flipping over a trump card
"Look! Look at his middle name!
I've never seen that before!"
With his sister, he guffawed
and flapped his prize, swatting
the laughs not to bring attention.
Youngest, left out, did a goalie's spring
to reach, but "Here, have a look!"
Quickened by guilt he read "Fitzgerald"
and it stuck, a curious nickname.

Tea-time was Fitzgerald's occupation
of the kitchen and the youngest
shrank his mam to a key-hole
as she spooned veg he couldn't name,
a waitress at the shoulder.
Unfamiliar and exotic smells gushed
through the door and their talk
went side to side, not in competition
but like levels of a building.
He thought of the earlier mockings
and wanted to be part of them,
to put in window-frames, to set
a river and pasture scene.

That was the year Kennedy died.
The older ones saw it on television
and expected the lodger to realise
the prophecy of his name and go away
with his suitcase full of samples,
leaving his collection of bottles
and their heavy hints of seduction.

But he remains there sitting, napkin tucked;
inflated from all her indulgence,
condensation covering his specs as their mam
crouches at the door, spying into a hall
of vanished children and letters falling.

Middle Age

Middle-age is when
you begin to get sensitive
about the crowd swearing at bald ref's.

It's when you daughter's
History homework's on Dunkirk
and she asks "Were you around then?"

You look in the mirror every morning
glad that you're short-sighted
and haven't got your glasses on.

Certain nouns slip out of memory
to be replaced by verbs
like "to sleep" and "to lie".
It's when you want time
to go rapidly to the next holiday,
yet halt completely before you die.

It's when your appalling flatulence
is exposed to your spouse
and you don't even bother to say "Pardon!"

You acquire irritable and incurable
ailments in corners of your body
and consider using herbal remedies.

You decide you need a new challenge:
working without a tie, your naked
adam's apple is swallowed by the boss's eyes.

Middle-age is when you take yourself for granted:
treat your dreams as pieces of furniture,
get rid of them on a skip.

It's when you're addicted to routine
and you won't admit it, keep on taking it
till you O.D. on those same old scenes.

Famous Player

Larger than television
he'd drink anyone
under the floor,
gathered around him
like family and fire,
waiting on every word
the smell of scandal
stronger than draught beer:
a holiday and setting fire
to women's knickers
the team behaving just like
any other slobby trippers,
obsessed with the size of plonkers
and dubious strikers
who could go either way.
The chairman's an asset-stripper,
the manager's his dummy,
but he's City till he leaves
to sell his kicks
across the market-fields.
He talks fan-lingo
he was there when it "went off"
at Bristol, as though
the fighting were a bomb
someone else had planted.
He's bigoted then liberated
spitting "bent" and "racist"
in a single sentence,
shrunk in his shoes
we just begin to argue
as he gets up to go.

Psychodahlia

Down in the darkest corridors of municipalia
is where the seed must've come from,
nurtured no doubt by a quirky computer
about the time of the Garden Festival.

It was to be Merthyr's own shrub:
a plant ideally suited to the area,
only needing to be oiled every ten years,
never losing its metallic beetroot colour.

"What should we call it?"
discussed the Parks committee:
"Mini triffid?" "Spike drunkard?"
"Ow about an ever 'ard?"

Without realising their irony,
because a stalwart councillor, after too many beers,
slipped on his way to a spaghetti
and skewered himself on the cast-iron cactus!

"DESTROY KILLER PLANTS!" screamed the local press,
but law and order merchants were impressed
by its vicious leaves and bought thousands
to surround the Civic Centre, schools and institutions.

Soon the forked flora had spread everywhere
threatening the soles of stray vandals,
so the Council named it "Psychodahlia"
and the computer was made into mayor.

Gurnos Shops

An emaciated tree
clinging to its blackened leaves,
the wind snuffles chip-cartons.

The road's an aerial view
of dirt-dragging streams,
its scabs peeled off by tyres.

Clouds collect exhaust-fumes.
A man takes his beer-gut for a walk,
his wife follows on a lead unseen.

They won't climb up on plinths
where benches ought to be
and pose like shop-dummies.

Lamp-posts droop their nightly heads,
strays will do the watering.
Graffiti yells, but nobody's listening.

Yr Wyddfa Speaks Out

It's summer again
and trip-trap trailing termites
carrying their backpacks
tread me down
sporting "I've climbed Snowdon"
t-shirts: who's this "Snowdon" anyway,
some kind of Lord?

It's rack and pinion all the way
the bumper to bumper
wanderlust like humping Nature
from grassy foothills
to flushes of heather;
get away from city-life
and breathe in fresh steam
laced with redhot cinders.

Oh! Not again! Here comes
the birdwatcher with two black eyes
jutting out, the silly old buzzard
hovering on an edge for hours
in his khaki plumage.

And there's nothing more boring
than a geomorphologist
labelling me with terms
like arrêtes and U-shaped valleys,
as the light changes
he's too busy turning pages.

Look at that snap of photographers
trying to suck the scenery
into those extended noses,
if I had the power to bring fog
swirling around my summit
to confound their art, I'd do it.

Those campers with butterfly nets,
at least they linger
to get moist with the dew
I perspire, try to listen
to my heart whose sounds
fall down to lakes, where my reflection
swims towards another winter.

This House, My Ghetto

It might as well be curfew here:
the pubs I can't enter any more.
It was "Paki! Paki!", looks
like jagged, cut-throat glass
and "You stink!"
from knuckled whites of eyes.

I was born in this town,
passed the old hospital when walking home.
I know how a girl must feel:
every stranger a criminal,
every sleight of hand a reach for steel.

The night's no camouflage:
I recall my uncle's shop,
black letters of loathing
branded across its front.
My brother and I flung like tyres,
our flesh slashed like rubber
"You don't belong... fuck off home!"
Their spittle slugging my face.

I know how a girl must feel:
even in daylight the enemy
is the man who follows and a gang
ahead sends thoughts twitching.
Those bruises, insults, that blood
has stained my voice so it jitters.
Tall gate and drive, my watching window:
this house is my ghetto.

The Talking Shop

In the Talking Shop
they spit out bones
which an auxiliary sweeps up:
they're crushed and made into gloss
for the latest glamorous brochure.

They talk white paint, plush curtains,
flowers and plants in the foyer:
they shred leaves of Chaucer
to garnish an exhibition.

Cogs of paper push hands
and a clock somewhere
justifies its existence.
They decide to decide later.

All the pounds left over
from multi-gym exertions
are heaped on the floor
for clients to sketch
in their frequent boredom.

In the Talking Shop
originality is a luxury
nobody can afford:
and if you complain
the word-detectives soon arrest
your mouth and use it to bin
the scraped paint, dead flowers, shoddy curtains.

Catalogue for Those Who
Think They Own Everything

NASA space spectacles enable you
to see the holes in the ozone layer
as they're forming and automatically
filter out the ultra-violet rays.

Acid rainproof ponchos with litmus lining
which changes colour according to levels;
no fumble lightswitch, no stain bedding,
less pressure lamp, tranquillising window-blinds.

Peel fruit in five seconds, polish toilet-bowl in ten,
tape that mends everything, including a broken heart;
six beautiful chokers in one as worn by Princess Di.,
talk-back plants pioneered by her husband.

Multi-vac octopus suckers for cigarette smoke,
annoying insects and the neighbours' children;
a clothes shaver, a sock de-odifier,
anti-slip shoe-grip gets rid of paranoia.

A giant helping hand for gardeners,
an extension on your penis, double-glazing for skin;
a drain buster, pet disguster, philosopher's knot,
an electric device for clearing nostrils of snot.

Learn a new language for just £5.95,
write a haiku for less than one pound;
detect radar zones over a mile away
and avoid crashes with low-flying planes.

Sonic lawn guarder repels moles harmlessly,
magnetic birds' mess collector keeps washing free;
"Don't Let The Bastards Get You Down" ties,
thermal pants with an "Up Yours!" motif.

Walk on water — insoles to match Christ!
A revolution in home heating — who needs Marx?
Oxygen in a can, feel young in magic minutes,
no needles, no wax.... ALL MADE IN BRITAIN.

Searching the Doll

Slowly pacing the beach
in age now not in sleep,
it's a cemetery
but I've come to dig.
Gulls wailing what's inside.

I'm alone again at night
in a walking trance
searching for that doll
I dropped, the blood-smirch
on its white wedding-dress.

My prints always lead back
to the cellar of that house.
A nine-month sentence stretched
to life on its camp-bed:
the memory condemned.

I chatted so readily then,
hadn't learnt suspicion's martial art,
his affection the breath of air
and hands soft as powdery sand.
Soon became my jailer, my interrogator.

Buried me under his sweaty bulk
so my frenzied fingers tried
to take flight and reach up
to the single slit of light.
Dead birds washed up with the flotsam.

Vedran Smailovic

People dash across our TV screens
like sheep scatting from a moorland blaze,
they'll disappear over the edge of dreams
when we ascend to sleep away the day.

But, all of a sudden, within a frame,
a portrait animated and tightly-strung:
the cellist plays on streets where lame
buildings hobble before falling down.

His slashback hair is aging rocker style,
upturned moustache makes a sign of peace;
his two faces: a pizzicato smile
and mournful vibrato of so much grief.

His audience are the pavement wreaths,
from the distance come heckles of gunfire:
the amphitheatre where he once bowed
is a frozen skip of bricks and wires.

On a thin point he gradually spins
the web-fine veins of an Adagio,
while hearing the bombs' deadening dins
and fearing for that small bridge below.

The Ghost Boy

for John Davies

Until this I did not believe:
thinking it a figure of speech,
product of too many spirits
or, simply, the heart
catching up with the mind.
Though there'd been inklings
in strange places or
                    openings in dreams.

Here, he came as I lay
facing the ceiling,
                    vivid
without sunlight
                    he stood
at the end of the bed.

Mustard-flower hair in a sash
across his forehead
                    enquiring politely
what I wanted... "Water?"
I shook myself awake
with a horse's snortling.
His one word kept repeating
"Water... Water... Water?"
Parched, but I didn't drink again.
Childishly switched a light on.

Once a farmhouse with doors
in all directions
                    once a cafe
for serious walkers
                    the boy
waited within original stone,
his spring tone
                    sipped by finches
observing me though a glass cage
where I sat munching.

81

Dŵr

Clouds —
whole valley-sides covered in berries
ripe and ready for the picking,
a steep rock-face with overgrown heather,
a flock of black sheep running
to be rounded up and sheared by the wind:
water with its roots in the sky.

Rain —
the drizzly seeds of droplets sown,
the slanting sea-strewn westerlies
which turn clothing to blotting paper,
the aching storms which gravel
into bones, making you shrink and cower.

Valleys —
scooped and scoured out by laws,
people cleared away like shanty-dwellers
bossed by bulldozers, memories
left to night-writers, to bells
tolled by feeding streams and rivers,
to drought and dereliction exposed.

Reservoirs —
acid funnels of the conifers
press down soil to stop it slipping;
to trippers they seem like mirrors,
but they balance water on scales
tapping mountains for its wealth.

Pipelines —
over the border, moving like a train
with trucks of coal, like iron and steel
liquid and molten, like the feet
of all those who had to leave
muttering "Money, money..." forced
against the gradient, longing for sea.

Chemicals —
a layer of aluminium the surface sheen,
the weight of lead its depths
and those substances meant to purify
unseen in a clear glass, lurking like radiation.

Houses —
the old person whose grasp of time
runs through knotted fingers and down the drain,
children whose minds become stagnant;
families knowing when it's cut off
water's precious as air when they choke
on the stench of their own cack,
as germs breed cockroaches and rats.

Dŵr —
they've stolen the word, those safe-lock faces,
mispronounced it "Door", reinforced and vaulted
below reservoirs where they've counted
profits from broken bones of village walls,
from a thirst which opens mouths
in fledgling questions to the clouds.

from
Graffiti Narratives

Mouthy

Sborin, sir!
We're always doin racism.
It's that or death, sir.
Yew're morbid, yew are,
or gotta thing about the blacks.

But sir mun! Carn we do summin intrestin
like Aids or watch a video o' Neighbours?
Mrs Williams Media upstairs ave got 'em.

Oh no! Not another poem!
They're always crap, rubbish
not enough action, don' rhyme.

Yer, sir, this one's got language in it!
It's all about sex!
Yew're bloody kinky yew are!
I'm gettin my Mam up yer.

Sir! We aven done work frages,
on'y chopsin in groups.
We ewsed t'do real English
when we woz younger,
exercises an fillin in gaps.

Sir mun! don' keep askin me
wha we should do,
yew're the bloody teacher!

Among the Debris

Ee were a brill teacher, ee were.
Ewsed t'tell us stories
of is time in the navy.
Playin cards underwater
is leg trapped in a giant clam.

But ev'ry so often
ee'd go mental, throw a wobbly,
grabbin ower desks an chairs
as we woz scibblin appily
an fling em flyin
is eyes explodin like gas,
is screams pick-axin
into ower yer-drums,
ower mouths woz gulpin,
we wuz so stunned!

An arfta, ee always passed
a bagfull o' sweets round,
tellin us ow ee still
could yer that sound:
a slow, unnatural thunder
of movin ground an ow
ee wuz searchin fer them lost children,
burying is ands in slurry
till ee found us, sittin
among the debris.

Valleys Veteran

See this medal, mun?
Ad it fer asslin-a Paddies,
searching-a Micks,
uprootin ouses, dirty tricks.

See these engravin's, my name?
Like a minted coin it is,
ne' mind the Queen.
wish I could spend it though —
carn do nothin now,
got buggerall compensation.

In a right ole we woz,
lovely barb-fire fencin
an women galore... on walls:
plenty o' one and dancin.

Musta bin darft or summin:
in cadets they tol us
the IRA wired up babies.
But I seen my butty
like a butcher's window in seconds.

Got my leg from-a Falklands —
a little souvenir, see?
From shaggin too many penguins!

Naa! The bloody Sir Galahad!
Well, we wuz on'y Taffies,
'ey shifted ammunition 'fore us:
we wuz left in-a ship's pit
like canaries before 'n explosion
with-a stink of ower fear
worse 'n cack from-a Phurnie.

Eero? Well, I never seen us win,
arf-dead in ospital I woz —
ne' mind gold, I'm a man o' tin.

Once a Musical Nation

I'm tellin yew theyr off theyr trolleys!
A whool famlee o'nutters!

I seen em through a gap
in ower Vesuvian blinds
with all theyr comin's an goin's:
I'd rather them Rastafarasians
smokin... what-yew-call... grass 'n'leaves.

They play in the street
with all the kids (cept owers, o'course):
I think they're mentally efficient.
Course, I never let em ave theyr ball back,
just t' teach em a lesson.

They d' play piano loud ev'ry evenin
as ower baby's goin off, what timin.
They sing in Welsh an all:
I'm shewer they belong
to them Sons of Glenfiddich.

Why carn they ave a satellite saucer
like ev'ryone else? There's effin 'n'blindin,
it's all in my diary, written down.
An even theyr anky-panky sounds
like a cage o' monkeys.

We're Merthyr born 'n' bred.
They come from bloody Aberdare!
They don' pay theyr poll tax
an let off fireworks in the New Year.

I'm tellin yew, we're goin off our trolleys
now theyr eldest's learnin violin.
We ave t' turn up ower telly...
an t' think, we woz once a musical nation.

Goin Fast

I gorra tell yew, sir mun,
carn keep it in no more:
now I seen er goin fast
like one of them pooer Ethiopians.

See, I know wha's up with er,
ow she've tried t' tell ev'rybody,
specially yew oo've bin ev'rywhere:
I think she fancies yew secretly.

It's er ol fella, see.
Aye, I know er famlee seem ordinree,
but I don' believe
in them words no more really.

Well... ee've ad er... y'know, sir...
reg'lar like ee wuz fishing,
she feels an ook inside er:
ev'ry pound she loses coz of 'im.

An I ave t'say, coz yew care...
wha cun we do? It's like on a telly
an she've come outa the screen:
she's killin erself an I on'y stare.

Singles Night

It's Singles Night at-a local
all-a women burst in like snow
an the baldy specky D.J.
carn wait t' play em real slow.

The last D.J. wuz a dick'ead
with-a tact of a J.C.B.:
playin "Stand By Yewr Man" and "She's Leavin Ome"
with-a demolition subtlety.

The women buzz o'perfume
the men got sideboards from M.F.I.,
even-a walls are sweatin,
everyone's givin the eye.

A piss-artist Social Worker
carn believe wha ee's seein:
all is clients gathered together,
ee ead-butts the telly screen!

"Fuck yew!" she yells, "I wouldn!"
she's coarse as wire wool.
There's more ex's than on-a coupon,
everyone's on-a pull.

It's Singles Night at-a local,
the Social Worker's lost is ands;
couples leave in wrestlin olds,
loners go ome t'finger stands.

Now I'm Sixteen

Well, I come in late
coz I wuz up-a Park
watchin the fight an coppers come
an I lost my watch runnin

an now I'm grounded

my Mam seen me smokin
by-a shops an I tol er
she smokes anyway
the silly ol cow

and now I'm grounded

we nicked a pram
an pushed it down-a sliproad
jus missed a Juggernaut
give my pissed brother a lift ome

an now I'm grounded

my Dad caught me snoggin
by-a bus-stop with this lush boy
oo woz over-age, ee says
yew'll get Aids, yew slag!

an now I'm grounded

me an 'is boy Darren
(they do call im Dazzy)
went to a party
an smoked wacky-backy

an now I'm grounded

I run away to stay
with my best friend Debbie,
but my parents come an grabbed me
saying they'd kick me out nex birthday

an now I'm grounded

I swallowed forty magies
ad my guts pumped dry,
woke up in Prince Charles
to a diet o' runny jelly

an now I'm grounded

I smashed a bottle on theyr borin telly
an yelled if 'ey grounded me agen
I'd turn into a friggin Jumbo Jet!
an they called me rotten

an now I'm sixteen.

New Poems

Stations Past Ponty

for David Hughes

All along the railway tracks
at the stations past Ponty
you see them: sports gear and baseball caps,
off their faces, out of their heads
the boys and girls, the not-so-teens
fuckin' this and fuckin' that
across the lines not caring what
the signal is, aiming cans
at cheeky pigeons, screeching
at a lone woman, target practice,
having a laugh and dropping tabs...
till Merthyr Vale and one's flat out
knocked out by some noxious cocktail
of cheap brew and stray prescriptions,
over him two cops are grinning
and taking notes from anxious mates.
Nobody's reviving him, he's lying
like a corpse at the scene
of a crime, the culprit's inside:
the van's on its way, ambulance siren
not heard... breath doesn't fall or rise.
The train moves on to another station,
another shelter where there is none.

Merthyr People

for Steve Phillips, photographer

Waltzing Eyes

She's framed by the Zimmer, knits her arthritic fingers into
each other, the crotchety texture of her pain.
The present is a tea-cup (no saucer), the stump of a candle,
an egg-cup full of pins.
Further along the mantelpiece the dice are all on one, a
photo of her grandchildren burnt white by her cataracts.
It becomes darker: her hubby's trophy, his leather-bound
portraits a modest library.
Her skin is falling. At her feet are neatly-chopped logs. If
she should rub her bones much harder, then a spark....
There's smoke from her grey hair. If only her flesh were
grained like wood.
Behind her shoulders the plant has turned to soot.
You won't see her waltzing eyes till the flames begin.

Wolf Hour

It's wolf-hour in the precinct: pack of dogs, pack of boys. The
mirror can't be seen. They reflect and swop
features, triads with sharpened fangs.
Leaders face nose to snout, staring each other out.
Three concrete blocks where winners would stand to
receive a battered coke-can cup.
The dogs are more patient: paw-leafed pavingstones
are their horizons.
The boys have blurry feet. One jerks in incredible
contortions, head taking off over the binned estate.
Hip-hop away, their leader's flung a can — "Fuckin mangy
strays! Don' shit yer!" His hair thick as an alsatian's coat.
It's wolf-hour in the precinct: the Shop Boys lurk in the
background, from a ridge of reputation. Night comes,
they'll snap up and pocket the silver moon.

Shadow Without Sun

Perched on a black and white pillar, call him "Piggy", he
doesn't care. His head's two stories above his sister.
His knee jabbers for him, saying: "I'm loud 'n' dirty, I'm
bloody mucky, open t' the air."
Arms folded, captain of a team of one, holding the match
ball, his cheeks blown up.
He's casting a shadow without the sun. She's in it, clutching
her check skirt in case the wind.... Her hair's the shine of a
plastic bucket.
Her face conceals a window. His hair is curtained,
tousled, already drawn.

Paper Escapes

Little black books
like school bibles
easy to hand
shiny as guns
telling how.to. punctuate.
if it's not written down
it doesn't exist
if in doubt
fill in a form:
marching columns
Roman legions
castle crenellations
a plan for life
no yellow-sprayed hair
no graffiti's sprawl
no rings in noses
no Pucker Georges:
polished as a scream
the set-off fire-alarm's
ear-splitting up-yours
when catches break
opening like hand-cuffs
and paper blows
(tons of it)
with November leaves
becoming itself and screeing
down the banks, through
the sun-sluicing fence,
away across the estate
like the end of the year.

Moithered

She used it totally out of place
but natural as calling an infant "Babes!"
The poet's moithered by all that pollution
like herself annoyed at my constant questions.

The word was *her*, chewing-gum twirler
giving so much lip and jip,
a desk-scribbler stirrer
using her tongue as a whip.

It was perfect for *flustered*:
I could imagine the artist
as all the complex phrases whirred
and churned, his hair in a twist.

No examiner could possibly weight it,
no educationalist glue and frame it:
it leapt out like her laughter
and my red mark was the real error.

A Lesson in Parrots

"I've forgotten my sheep-pig!" she announces.
"Oh, so you've got one as well?
They must be catching on."
Knock on the door, here's a likely....
"Miss Frostrup needs three parrots."
"Haven't got any, " I tell him,
"nasty squawky things, live in cages."
Handing him three stolen biros
placed in my drawer by Alun
the stubby, smelly pen-thief
with tall, highly-perfumed mother.

"Can I go to the tortoise, sir?"
asks Sam, authentically hopping.
"Yes, but don't drown the turtles."
I hand her a plastic toilet pass
which will return dripping.

"Where's Jay today? Anyone?"
I expect them to say
she's in the woods with her gang,
but there's yet more knocking.
"Can Mr Jones have some tipex?"
"The ibex is extinct in this room."
The girl on the message runs away
like an antelope chased by a jaguar.

One parrot is brought back
(apparently it failed to talk)
and I send Miss Frostrup another
that swears blue, with a beak
like a Bic. Come summer
when ants troop through my windows,
beasts will be banished from my room.

Wee Maeve

She was eleven, freckly-faced and gingery-hair
sharp in class as the skrake of dawn,
chubbily confident amongst wild, wiry boys
who — knowing only mastery of the cane —
spent more time on the floor than sitting down.

I took quicker to the rounded vowels
of her Christian name, Maeve (an Irish queen)
than the baffling silents of the likes of Siobhán
and her surname, Connolly, had all
the ricochets of their history:
the executed martyr... how so much began.

One day she explained a rare absence
every word noted carefully, she taught us
more than I ever could, struggling for a say.
I imaged wee Maeve shocked awake,
her door battered down, the Para's invading
her home, dragging her Da away.

In that commonplace classroom in Clady
it was hard to see how she'd kicked out
and scrabbed such burly armed men,
must've brushed her aside like a pesty fly.
She described her revenge intricately:
mirror to the eyes of the helicopter pilot
targeting with her weapon, the sun.

Bethesda Brought Down

While the new road arcs
around measures waiting to be blown
and struts above roofs of terraces;
while the fountain's poshed
and the Korean factory's built
fast as the street's demolished.

Gone the potter's wheel where hands
made shapes which browned like loaves;
gone the dark room where prints
grew and bloomed with voices
meeting Parry's spirit in organ-pipes
of poem and song.

Bethesda brought down —
the civic vandals strike again,
each shattered stone a script torn,
only the Holm Oak protected by bars.
In the nearby office signers-on
are portraits framed by forms
and every season is angry now:
the east wind carries no applause.

The Farmers Released

Farmers ran wild like released mink,
they were deadly dangerous predators,
their canines filed and sharpened,
everything in their way
was attacked and knocked down,
pet-photographers ran for their lenses,
otter-jotters hid behind lorries,
the farmers were a liability
to everyone and themselves,
if they couldn't hunt down Ministers
then they'd turn on Junior officials
ravaging brief-cases, ties
in their jaws as they swung
the hapless bureaucrats
like mice caught by cats.
Who had freed them
from the captivity of hill cottages,
the surety of dry-stone walls?
They need to be netted,
binned, returned to domesticity
and penned by high fencing
till they could be skinned
and sold, a tourist's luxury.

Punishment Victim

Like a child learning to walk again
with a false leg,
limb made of lead:
he drags it along
weighty as cross or ball-and-chain,
all of his concentration
past the Sheltered Accommodation,
old young man, darkly handsome,
could be a famous face
elsewhere, but here
the kneecap uniform
they made him wear
conscripted pain
of "What do you expect?"
or "He's only to blame!"
What wheel or needle
or just a roll of herbs
in those hands deserved this?
The street-police hiss,
kerbstones press his sole,
delicate as a baby's skull.

The Wrong Rain

It rained for weeks on end
the whole holidays and beyond,
the monsoon season came to the Valleys
and, for once, the Tories weren't to blame!
Like upturned beetles, umbrellas lay
by roadsides and my back lawn
was a lodging for passing geese.
In England, entire villages were saturated
and caravans washed away
like twigs downstream.
Newsreaders were momentarily horrified
by stories, like the old woman
drowned as she was sleeping.

Yet the water authorities
still warned of future drought:
"It's the wrong rain," they explained
with no further elaboration.
Evidently, this was rain like leaves
falling on railway tracks to stop
the system, H20 which went
in all the wrong directions.
This was undrinkable, unthinkable rain
the sort that needed marching
down lead pipes, into our brains.

Skylark and Violinist

I

"Just listen to the skylark!" he said
as we stood on the iron-ore spoil-tips
reclaimed by crackling, sinewy heather.
Its song rose into a blueness
without a trace of the bird
as if reed and fern were singing.
"Derelict land!" we mocked official description
as three boys held fishing-rods aloft,
bobbing to the pond. Across valley
other reclamations were plasticky green
where occasional marauding crows
ventured (no whinberries or wildflowers).

II

She appears, you can watch her:
the lark made human,
her eyes turned upwards,
fingers feather trills.
Pauses, silences of the air
also music as the bird breathes
before her playing ascends towards
the flight-paths to America.
Orchestra are soil and seams,
but we are taken higher,
losing horizon-lines of her score:
no boundaries between sky and moor.

Rehearsing After the Play

She's rehearsing, but the play has ended. Stripped of the costumes: pink of motley, red of tragic queen.
Telephone uproots her nerves, flowers with wires dangling. Her voice without bloom is a pencil-line stem: tentative as her heart-beat when a draught burgles in.
She's rehearsing on the plush velvety sofa, the windows becoming wooden: lying for their fit.
He measures her up with knife and fork, brings a tray to pin her down.
Her diet of pills rattle the brass knocker. They scour out her insides, stuff her with dead leaves, embalm her with tannin.
"My hair's falling! My skin's like bark! I want to see no-one!"
She once talked to her garden gnomes. He resembles them. Glum, she'd call him.
Her nails are long enough for hammering.

Moor Snake

Seems to swim through grass
soundless foot-long whip,
afraid of us, then still
except its forked tongue,
flicking sticking-pad
for crane- and dragon-flies,
its eyes two points of light
on butterflies, its white
marking a mask slipped.

A curve of leaden colour
with tail its pencil tip,
not camouflaged one bit
across the marshy moor,
kestrel and buzzard, spy and claw;
autumn's fern cover far away,
one false move betrays
itself, the silent s's
at the end of our fears.

The Scout

He even watches the pre-match kickabout,
his walking-stick poking a stray ball.
It's a perfect day for the passing game,
sunny September early season,
dew silvery as trophies,
new nets orange as half-time segments.

His village has gone with the landslip,
Troedrhiwfuwch's not even a sign:
he talks proudly of nine professionals
from there, who must've been
every other son, a rough patch
on the hillside, mud-strewn.

The little player who's forgotten his boots
asks "Are you scouting for Watford?"
"No! Much bigger than that."
He remembers Welsh League matches, reffing
and horse-cropped fields like the Bont.

His suit must also have been there
as he plucks old stars from annuals,
"Albert Quixall" the only one I recognise.
He shouts out tips to lads:
"Push it back!", "Look for space!"
gaps spotted by his astute eyes.

I wonder at the fact or fiction:
every boy looking up to him not thinking
of a sliding slope to dereliction,
only climbing steps to glory
as he waves that crooked wand.

The Pwll Massacre

We're playing high above the tundra zone
v. Pwll Boys' Club under 14's
on a pitch shared by sheep,
horse-riders, motorbike scramblers
and more dogs than Crufts.

We're in with a chance
till we count our team:
nine players including three keepers,
two of our star defenders
have discovered lager at 13
and there's no way to wake them.

Pwll are a small team
with the best (and only) oranges half-time.
They even have a tea-urn,
which is useful in the Arctic circle
somewhere north of Asda's.

We play a mystery formation
including at least seven strikers.
The pre-match team-talk involves
"It's a game of two halves,
but not equal players!"

It's their ref. and he's fair
as the weather. At 4-0 down
we're heading for their goal
only to be whistled for off-side...
our manager's warned for swearing,
their parents give him verbals
like snowballs packed with stones,
a collie brings light relief
with the most adept footwork
since Stanley Matthews....

At 12-0 down I give up counting:
the game's lost its point
because the local paper
only report the first ten!
We score a consolation
when the collie deftly noses in.
It's disallowed as he's underage
and anyway, hasn't signed the forms.

The ref. plays twenty minutes extra time
so his son can get a hat-trick.
Pwll parents are all gloating
like polar bears watching
a load of rabbits fishing.
"Ne' mind, son, " I say after,
"at sea level you'd have won!"

International Evening

Couple in the bank entrance take no account of anyone. Engrossed, entangled, she unzips him as if she'd peel a banana with two fingers. He clutches her yellow, leather skirt like a saddle. She's over-riding.

Cash machines open lit mouths, mechanical birds. Give bread: crusty notes soon sag.

The day's debris spewed over borders: cans, bottles, take-away wraps. Empty endings.

Time belongs to the young: girls strut in nightgear, boys in amplified ties. Spilled from pubs, the crowd stamp on flower-heads.

Later, there are gangs of men (collective noun: a discord), mauling each other, playing rugger with one's shoe and annihilating the best ballads with their noxious brew: the lace and the screw, the never-safe pair of hands.

Forbidden Words

based on a photograph by Philip Jones Griffiths

This was the war we never saw,
the hidden war —
the face that was kept
buried in the sand,
nose and lips bitten off
by the wind, hair and uniform
oily black, his eyeballs
returned to meet the gun.

This was the soldier once concealed
now every grain raises him up,
his teeth making a print
bolder than any headline.

The ammunition-case is no coffin,
the bombed-out truck no hearse,
yet cremation fires shoot
dark smoke into the horizon
as though setting fire
to the edges of earth.

His skin's a decaying parchment
telling forbidden words.

Woman in a Tree

There is a woman hanging in a tree.
She's been there too long
and nobody will let her down.
She has Queen Victoria's headdress,
high-heels and brown stockings.
She is hanging by her hair.
Her hips move gradually
back and fore; the oak's full
with leaves though summer whispers
in the ears of a cow
rubbing its buggy neck
against a trunk's bend.
There is a woman, her face
concealed or eaten away
by crows, I cannot tell
' who put her there or whether
she dangles in warning,
her body's amber gauze
trapped at the point of falling.

The Great Western

The Great Western laid to rest
in the dead centre, not far
from the barred precinct.
No puff left and the wheels
have long since rolled
down valley to Cardiff.

Above the bar, Sandie Shaw's feet
make whistles through tarry teeth
of regulars whose suits
are clinker and ash,
whose eyes refuse to light.

The big screen's bare
and hollow as a chimney,
the fag-machine has a hose
like a cooling pump.
On the sill's a packet of broccoli,
while BEEF's boldly chalked up.

Two spotlights are aimed
at a fan which is clogged
with dirt thick as coal-dust.
The window's a wire-webbed screen
into the High Street
where a couple of kids strut,
shut out in the dog-end dark.

The beer's strangely sweet
with a taste of sick or soap.
We tut at the evening's failures
ended here, with its ceiling
layered with years of smoke.

The Great Western in an engine graveyard,
as we three shovel and stoke
where tracks no longer remain
and the TV tunnel's beckoning back.

Snow Baby

You were a snow baby. We should've called you Eira. You were almost marooned in hospital: jaundiced face yellow as egg-yolk, clutched head the shape of a shell.

You grew to your name, Bethan, grew round. Your plum cheeks swelled to its sound.

And now in town you let the flakes settle in your long hair, saying "Ne' mind, I like 'em there."

I played you *Ommadawn*: layers of cloud, frost, hail and sun climbing till that lightning moment when you were born.

Wrapped still through frozen nights, layers of a nest taken from the strands of our house: broken violin string, discarded lace and strap of a watch you never wore.

Your dreams hatch and drift with feathers of the pillow-bird you believe in no more.

Three Observations of Geese

I

Geese are more powerful than horses.
When it comes to bread
they will spit worse
than any teacher or preacher,
the venom of their cobra-tongues
halting the young stallions
on the other side of the stream.
It's the noise of the whip,
of breaking in, which makes
strong animals bridle at the pair
of snaggling goose and gander.

II

Nobody can deny the pecking order.
Ferocious against each other,
beaks which snap shut
on wing-feathers, or jab
at eyes, the opponent's
shriek-honk of pain
sending them to the back
with the lame one and the other
whose call's still gosling-sharp.

III

Meticulous as cats they clean together
away from the web-waxy mud
on the tussocky moorland
they contort and pick
beaks now implements of relief,
till they sleep as one,
so quiet you could mistake them
for marbled boulders
left by an ancient ocean.

The Essence of Presents

Presents are all about revenge —
I send him Gerry Adams' latest volume,
he replies with an S.A.S. tome.

They're to do with humiliation —
the time I got given
grandad's rusted tin-opener as an heirloom.

They're about total disregard —
my omnivorous son once sent
a boxful of dried vegan fare.

They're meant to baffle —
that plastic mosquito-net for cheese
we longed to use, but never quite....

Presents are about forgetting ages —
as when my teenage daughter
received a second-hand Maths textbook.

And those telling phrases when giving —
like "I've read it, it's really good.
In fact, it's the same one!"

Essentially they're about re-cycling —
that familiar wallet which does the rounds,
that bargain scarf I found.

Above all, they're about being grateful
that most of those kindly people
live too far away for a sly "Thank you!"

The Tap Plays a Perfect A

As my son plays Albinoni's *Adagio*, the shine on his bow a fragile skin of light before we go; nerve-strings tense before flight into what, how can we know? The wood no coffin, but a boat sailing without wind, with the air of sound.

On a perfect *A*, the house echoes. We don't know where the note's reply comes from at first. As if a ghostly instrument....
" Tune by the tap in future, not the fork!"

So used to cold water train-tracks, we are aghast!

No turn of hand could repeat.... while the mast-head disappears from view: a grown child leaving home.

Tom Waits Blues

I think of you, *wasted and wounded*,
dragging yourself through the snow
to the porch below my flat,
a lame, lone stray in a strange country.

You'd left your marks of blood,
scattered petals of a thrown bouquet.
You'd licked those wounds, the grit
making you growl, your throat the street.

You were a dog-wind under the door,
a howl that shook the panes,
you were the half-empty bottle
I waltzed with, the beaten-up couple
who out-yelled the elements
from upstairs. The New Year fireworks
lay sodden, but I sang along
till my fingers clawed the grooves
following the curve of the shining circle.

(Rheinberg, Germany)

"wasted and wounded"
from Waits' song *Tom Traubert's Blues.*

Coastal Defences

You can see them on the map:
black dots outlining the southern coast,
ring after ring of fortification.
For each one: eyes of a kingdom,
the eyes of cannons,
the belly of King Henry,
the stout gunpowder barrels.

The English on their beaches
knock in stakes with stones,
not a sniff of breeze
but they surround their families
with windbreaks for fear of being exposed.

Down on the flat sand
children assist their fathers
in that serious business
of castle-building, turrets and walls
face the waves and invasion.

Four flags placed: above a deep moat
the Union Jack and to its side
on smaller towers, red dragon, harp and lions.
The banners are saved before the tide
comes rapidly in, innocently conquering.

His Last Demonstration

He stands to demonstrate for the last time. From his office not the dark room brings a negative of his midriff. His bones pounded to chalkdust, stomach an unfinished graffiti mark.

There is no symmetry. His hands try to re-create the sawn-off hip-bone, moulding as he won't at the wheel again. The air leaves nothing. We imagine a drill carving him up, making an imperfect sculpture.

It will never be developed, will stay pegged, to drip away his time.

On a plinth of books a yellow melon looks artificial, fit to be duplicated in still life drawings.

"...as long as I've got." His spare leg propped, new feet only for the flat.

He can add no primaries to this smoky X-ray. Outlines of skin a vain sketch. Single hip a caricature angel.

His upright beliefs left in shades of red on his face. Eyes — brown rodents — retreat to earth.

A Heron Flies Overhead

In the scatterings of the year
the clothes will not take flight,
twigs and leaves do not stir
and the moor fades out of sight.

A tree-creeper scurries against gravity,
two jays are flowers of the air,
the geese snake water thirstily,
magpies are always asking "Where?"

A heron flies overhead with calm
and rhythmic pulsing of the wings,
towards the west it charms
my senses with its rare passing.

It seems now like a prophecy:
what will happen when streams have gone?
Diggers will treat the mountain ruthlessly,
fumes and dust consume the songs.

Acknowledgements

These poems were published in individual Seren collections: *The Common Land* (1981), *Empire of Smoke* (1983), *Invisible Times* (1986), *A Dissident Voice* (1990), *this house, my ghetto* (1995). *Graffiti Narratives* (1994) was published by *Planet*.

Acknowledgements are due to the editors of the following publications, where some of these poems first appeared: *The Anglo-Welsh Review, Borderlines, Encounter, Envoi, Cencrastus, Chapman, Cumberland Poetry Review, The Chariton Review, Fortnight, Hybrid, The Independent, NER/BLQ, New Statesman, New Welsh Review, The North, The North Dakota Review, Planet, Poetry Ireland Review, Poetry Wales, Prospice, Quartz, Radical Wales, Red Poets' Society, Smoke, Spectrum, Staple, Welsh Nation, Willliwaw,Working Titles, The Works, Y Faner Goch.*

The new poems have previously appeared in the following publications: *Borderlines, Cambrensis, The Chariton Review, Cencrastus, Encounter, Envoi, Fortnight, The Interpreter's House, New Hope International Forum, The New Welsh Review, Planet, Poetry Wales, Red Poets' Society, Staple, Y Faner Goch.*

Recent anthologies include: *Christmas in Wales* (Seren), *The Bright Field* (Carcanet), *The Valleys* (Poetry Wales), *The Streets and the Stars* (Seren), *Coal* (Seren), *Love from Wales* (Seren), *Wales in Verse* (Secker and Warburg), *Burning the Bracken* (Seren), *An Idea of Bosnia* (Feed the Children), *The Heart of Wales* (Seren), *The Urgency of Identity* (Triquarterly Books), *Anglo-Welsh Poetry 1480-1980* (Seren), *Poetry Wales 25 Years* (Seren), *Are You Talking To Me?* (Pont), *The Welsh Academy School Resources Pack.*

A number of these poems have been broadcast on the BBC, HTV and radio.